"There have been in. ... isms of love, almost all contained in the supreme radi... Christ Jesus. There has been the radicalism of Francis of Assisi, of Ignatius of Loyola, of Charles de Foucauld and many others up to our days. There is also Chiara's radicalism of love . . . a radicalism which discovers the depth of love and its simplicity, and discovers all the demands of love in different situations, and seeks to make this love victorious in every circumstance."

Pope John Paul II

"This woman is transparent like an open page of the gospel. I cannot forget that Chiara was chosen from the humble, the workers, in order to confound the strong, the powerful of this world. And I praise Christ our Lord for this."

Brother Roger Schutz of Taizé

"[Chiara Lubich is] a person who for decades has literally generated throughout the world countless apostles of peace, of reconciliation and of genuine Christian love: and this in a world often seen to be without God, irreparably secularized, egotistic, irreconcilable and desperate. From the first day of the Focolare Movement, Chiara Lubich took to heart the gospel of Jesus Christ and has prayed incessantly and has transmitted daily the message of unconditional love through her simple example."

Bartholomew I
Ecumenical Patriarch of Constantinople

"In an age when ethnic and religious differences too often lead to violent conflict, the spread of the Focolare Movement has also contributed to a constructive dialogue and creative interchange between peoples of different cultural backgrounds and religious faiths."

Paul Smoker
President of the UNESCO peace education jury
Professor of peace studies at Antioch College, Ohio

Chiara Lubich was born in Trent, Italy, in 1920, and in 1943 began what came to be called the Focolare Movement. Focolare now counts over 2 million members and adherents, and is present in more than 180 nations. Her work, especially her efforts in ecumenism and interreligious dialogue, has been rewarded with numerous recognitions and awards in the United States, England, France, Poland, Thailand, and the Philippines among others. Her international awards range from the Templeton Prize for Progress in Religion in 1977 to the UNESCO Prize for Peace Education in 1996.

In 1995 she was named the Author of the Year by the Italian Catholic Publishers Guild at the Milan Book Fair. She is the author of more than thirty books published in up to twenty-six different languages.

Christian
Living Today

Other Books in English by Chiara Lubich

Chiara Lubich

Christian Living Today

Meditations

New Translation and Edition

New City Press

Published in the United States by New City Press
202 Cardinal Rd., Hyde Park, NY 12538
©1997 New City Press

Christian Living Today—Meditations is translated from the twelfth edition
of the original Italian *Meditazioni* © Città Nuova Editrice, Rome, Italy.
This book first appeared in an English-language edition under the title,
The Christian Eye. Subsequent editions were entitled *Meditations*. The
current edition is translated by Julian Stead, O.S.B and Jerry Hearne.

Cover design by Nick Cianfarani
Cover photo by Gabriele Viviani

Library of Congress Cataloging-in-Publication Data:
A catalog record for this book is available from the Library of Congress
Library of Congress Catalog Number: 74-79452
ISBN 1-56548-094-5

7th printing: May 1997

Printed in the United States of America

Contents

Foreword

The writings in this book have long been considered spiritual classics. They have something in them for everyone. Readers who come upon them for the first time find themselves intrigued and delighted by their faith-filled wisdom. Ever since *Christian Living Today's* first publication, in fact, these meditations have been faithful companions on countless peoples' life journey. As we read and reread them, they speak to us in ever new ways.

This could be surprising given their apparent simplicity. Yet here we find a simplicity that contains sublime truths. A depth of meaning that gives us glimpses of another world. They express something of heaven's viewpoint that ultimately lies at the core of all our longings.

This "heavenly" perspective, however, can be drastically different from our usual way of reasoning about things and therefore not easy to grasp. While these life-giving words make the heart leap for joy and the spirit sigh with relief, they need to be put into practice for their full meaning to become clear.

The most common experience when reading these meditations is that they open up a dialogue with the Eternal, and the reader finds that a new logic, precisely that heavenly way of reasoning, begins to filter into the soul. We feel that we become better, and we discover a yearning, almost a homesickness, for heaven. And that turns us to face our everyday life and its many struggles with renewed resolution. We wish to care for others in the most realistic and down-to-earth way possible.

Indeed, we feel enabled to take part in fulfilling *Christian Living Today's* driving theme, the prayer Jesus summed up his life work with when he prayed to his Father the night before he died: "May they all be one" (Jn 17:21). In short, these meditations lead us on an adventure into God.

The Editor

Participants
in God's Plan
for Humanity

Today's Great Attraction

To reach the heights of contemplation,
   though still living side by side
      with all people,
finds great attraction in modern times.

I'd go further,
and blend with the crowd
infusing it with the divine
as wine that gradually soaks a piece of bread.

And further still,
as participants in God's plans for humanity,
weave light through the crowds
while sharing our neighbor's shame, hunger,
      troubles and brief joys.

For what has great appeal today
in ours as well as every age,
since we could hardly imagine
anything more human or more divine,
is Jesus and Mary:
the Word of God, a carpenter's son,
a housewife, the throne of Wisdom.

Fires of Love throughout the City

Suppose you started fires at various points in a city, even just modest ones, but fires able to defeat every attempt to extinguish them, in little time the whole city would be in flames.

If one were to kindle the fire Jesus has brought in widely different sections of the city, and the same fire overcame the freezing temperature of the world through the good disposition of the inhabitants, in not much time the whole city would be burning with God's love.

The fire Jesus came to bring on earth is himself, charity: The love which binds souls not only to God but also to one another.

In fact, the lighting of supernatural fire means a continual triumph for God in souls dedicated to him, united with him and consequently with one another.

Two or more persons united in Christ's name are a divine force in the world—if they are not only unafraid or not too embarrassed to openly declare to each other their longing to love God, but if they also make the unity among them in Christ the Ideal of their life.

Souls of this sort can emerge from the families of any and every city: mom and dad, son and father, daughter-in-law and mother-in-law; they can be found in parishes, associations and unions, schools, offices, everywhere.

They don't have to be saints already, or Jesus would have said so; it's enough that they are united in the name of Christ and never let this unity down.

Naturally, they will remain just two or three persons for only a short time, because charity is diffusive of itself, spreading itself in vast progression.

Small cells which God has lit at any points on earth will inevitably multiply. Divine providence will spread the fire of these soul-flames wherever it sees fit, so that more places in the world may be restored to the warmth of God's love and find new hope.

There is a secret whereby a burning cell can grow into tissue and bring life to some part of the mystical body: It is that those who compose it plunge into the Christian adventure by making every obstacle a springboard, not "putting up" with the cross whenever it comes, but looking forward to it and welcoming it from one moment to the next, as the saints do. When the cross comes, say: "This is just what I wanted, Lord! I know I belong to the Church militant, where one has to struggle. I know the Church triumphant is waiting for me there, where I will see you for all eternity. Here and now on earth I would rather suffer than anything, because you have told me, by your own life, that the greatest good lies there."

After saying yes to the Lord, the soul has to live the next moment to the fullest, without thinking of herself, of her own pain. Instead, she is to concern herself with the burdens of others she ought to carry with them, or with their joys she ought to share. At the same time, she must place all her mind's attention, her heart's affection, her energy and strength into fulfilling her own responsibilities, turning them into a continual prayer.

This is the little secret for building the city of

God within us and among us, stone by stone. Already here on earth it places us into God's will, which is God himself, eternally present.

Find Comfort
In Her
Love

Prayer To Saint Therese

Beloved Saint Therese,
Teach us how to pray
You show the world
unbounding love
In your "little way."
We sing to you, Our Little Flower,
and in return,
You send a shower
of Roses, to bless us on earth,
To show us God's grace and
Show us our worth
As children beloved of the
Father in Heaven.
Even in our darkest hour,
Let us never lose sight of
His Almighty Power.

Amen.

HOLY HILL

1525 Carmel Road
Hubertus, WI
53033-9407

©CM
DC40hc9

There Are No Thorns without a Rose

How sad to think of the lives of an awful lot of people that never get lived! They never live because they cannot see. They do not see because they look at the world, its objects, at their relatives, at everybody, with their own eye—whereas to see well, nothing more is needed than to follow each happening, every subject, every person, with God's eye. Those who graft into God see; knowing that God is love, they believe in his love, reasoning with the saints: "Everything God wills and permits is for my sanctification."

As a result, joys and sorrows, births and deaths, anguish and celebration, failures and victories, meetings, acquaintances, work, unemployment and sickness, wars and scourges, smiling babies, mothers' affection, all of it, all is prime matter for our sanctity.

Our lives are surrounded by worlds of every kind of value, the divine world, the angelic world, the world of the family, and even the hostile world, all disposed by God with a view to our deification, our true destiny.

Everyone is the center of this world, because love is its universal law.

For the sake of maintaining the proper human and divine balance, we must love. It is the will of the Most High that we always love both the Lord and our neighbor, what God wills and also what he permits. Then all people—knowingly or not—profit us. The changes in their existence are guided by love for us. It is a fact that everything cooperates for the good of those who love.

With our dim-sighted and incredulous eyes we very often cannot see how each and every one has been created as a gift to us, and we as a gift for them. But it is a fact. There is a mysterious bond of love binding people and things, guiding history, directing the outcome of the lives of peoples and individuals, while respecting freedom of the highest order.

As time passes, however, to the soul abandoned in God, and to whom "believing in love" is her law, God manifests himself; opening her eyes, she sees that she is drawing new benefits from every trial; every contest ends in victory, every tear develops into a new smile, new always because God is life, permitting the torments of evil for the sake of a greater good.

She understands that the life of Jesus does not reach its climax in the way of the cross, but at his resurrection and ascension into heaven.

Then the human style of looking at things loses its glamor and its sense, bitterness no longer spoils the brief joys of life on earth. The gloomy saying, "There is no rose without thorns," means nothing to her. On the contrary, as God sweeps her along on the crest of love's revolution, precisely the opposite has meaning: "There are no thorns without a rose."

The Diplomacy of Charity

When others cry, we ought to weep with them too. If they laugh, enjoy it with them. This way the cross is split up and borne on several shoulders, and the joy gets multiplied and shared in many hearts.

To make ourselves one with our neighbor is one way, the master way, to make ourselves one with God. The master way, because in this kind of charity the two first and chief commandments are fused: Making ourselves, for love of Jesus, one with our neighbor, [having] Jesus' love for our neighbor, so that our neighbor, having been gently wounded through us by God's love, will want to be one with us in a mutual exchange of help, ideals, projects and feelings: to a degree that the Lord may be able to say of us: "Where two or three gather in my name, I am in the midst of them" (Mt 18:20). All this to the point of guaranteeing the presence of Jesus so far as it depends on us, and of walking through life at all times like a church in miniature, as a church even at home, at school, in the office, in the legislature. Let us walk through life like the disciples on the way to Emmaus, with that Third between, who confers divine value on all we do. Then it will not be us who are living our lives, wretched and limited as we often are, lonely and in pain. The Almighty walks with us. Whoever abides in him bears much fruit. From one cell grow more cells, from one tissue comes more tissue.

Let us become one with our neighbor in that complete forgetfulness of self which takes over persons who think of others, of their neighbor— without self-consciousness or fretting about them. This is the diplomacy of charity. It finds expression in many of the ways of ordinary diplomacy. It does not blurt out all that it could, for instance, because one's neighbor would be displeased and so would God; it can wait, then speak up, and reach its goal. It's the divine diplomacy of the Word who became flesh to make us divine. There is something essential to it, nevertheless, and characteristic of it, differentiating it from what goes by that name in the world, where "diplomatic" is often synonymous with "reticent" or plainly "dishonest." What is great about divine diplomacy, unique to it perhaps, is its motivation for the good of the other and its consequent freedom from any taint of selfishness.

This is a rule of life which ought to characterize all diplomacy. With God's help it is possible, because he is not only each person's Lord, he is also the king of nations and of every human society.

If all diplomats were actually stimulated, in carrying out their proper functions, by care for the other state as well as for their own, they would be so illuminated by the grace of God that they could contribute to actualizing the sort of relationships between the states which ought to exist between people. Charity is a light and a guide, and if a person is sent on a mission he will receive all the graces necessary to fulfill it well.

May God grant us his aid. And let us so dispose ourselves that as he looks at us from heaven the Lord may see something new on earth: his will and testament actualized between the nations.

To us, this might seem a mere dream. For God, it is the normal thing, the only way to guarantee peace in the world, the empowerment of individuals in the unity of a humanity which has come at last to know Jesus.

One City Is Not Enough

If you wish to win a city over to the love of Christ, if you wish to transform some place into a kingdom of God, then you must first calculate the cost and draw up a plan.

Find some friends with the same desire. Unite with them in the name of Christ, asking them to be willing to sacrifice everything for God.

Make an agreement. Promise each other constant and perpetual love. That way the conqueror of the world will always be among you, leading. When love has destroyed your ego, the mother of great Love will uphold you at every step. She will wipe away all the tears and smile on you and your joys.

Then size up the city.

Go with your friends to meet its spiritual leader.

Explain your project and take no steps if your leader does not agree. Otherwise you would spoil everything. Any advice given and guidelines offered receive as a command. Let them be the watchword for yourself and your companions. On your part, express your devotion, for it is commanded by Christ. Offer your help and spiritual support in your leader's own grave responsibilities.

Then interest yourself in the most wretched people, in the homeless, the destitute, orphans, prisoners. With your friends, hasten to visit Christ in them. Comfort them ceaselessly, show them that God's love follows them and is near.

Bring food or clothes to those who need them.

If you have not any clothing or food to give, beg for them from the eternal Father. Tell him they are needed for Christ his Son, whom you want to serve in everybody. He will hear you.

Load up with goods and search the streets. Go up into attics or down into cellars. Look for Christ everywhere, in every place public or private, in bus or railroad stations, in slums, and especially greet him with your smile. Then promise him eternal love, for where you cannot go your prayers and your pains will arrive, united to the sacrifice of the altar.

Neglect no one. You can make them generous promises, for you come in the name of the Omnipotent.

While you cheer the Lord in your neighbor, he will take care to fill you and your companions with celestial gifts. Communicate them to each other, lest your light be extinguished and your love might stop flowing.

If you are firm, and your speech is seasoned with wisdom, many will follow you.

Divide these people into teams. With them you can leaven the city that you want to mine with love.

And keep on.

Others may hear of your life and come to see for themselves your gifts. If they ask you for an explanation, speak! But make the mainspring of what you say be what you have learned from life.

Let your speech reflect scripture and the thinking of the Church. You and your team will find there a safe, inexhaustible, eternal spring to drink from, your primary source. That way you will be the living expression of the shepherd's word.

When you have picked up those rejected by society, when you have helped and enlightened them, when you have given them happiness, you will have laid the foundations for the new city.

Then gather your companions and repeat the beatitudes to them, lest they ever lose the sense of Christ and of his preferences.

Widen then your horizons and tell everybody that each neighbor passing by is Christ, rich or poor, handsome or ugly, gifted or not.

Put your team at their service, Jesus and Mary's team, weeping with those who weep, rejoicing with those who rejoice.

Constantly share both happiness and sorrows. Never give up. No sacrifice could be too great.

Intersperse your activity with deep prayer, raised by your forces in perfect unison. Thus your town may win as much glory as possible for Christ.

If the struggle costs you dearly, know that this is the secret of success. He who is stimulating you paid with his blood.

Forgive, and pray for whoever opposes you. If you do not forgive, you will not find mercy yourself.

If you are consumed with pain, sing of your pain with the Song of Songs, "Such is my lover and such my friend" (5:16), so that when death arrives the Lord may say to your soul, "Arise, make haste, my love, my dove, my beautiful one, and come" (2:10). All this for the sake of one city, until it is conquered. That means until good has defeated evil, and through us Christ can say again, "I have overcome the world" (Jn 16:33).

But for the God who comes to visit you every morning if you like, only one city is not enough.

He made the galaxies of stars, he guides the centuries to their destiny.

Come to an agreement with him and aim farther, at your whole country, at everybody's country, the entire world.

Let your every breath be for this goal, for this your every move, your relaxation as well as your activity.

When you reach the next world, you will see what had the most value. You will be rewarded in proportion to how much you loved. Live now in such a way that you will not have to be sorry for having loved too little.

A Great Responsibility

We certainly have a great responsibility as Christians, because we must be witnesses for Christ. Others can conclude, from the way we live, what sort of message Jesus brought to earth.

Yet it sometimes happens that the testimony we give to Christ is little or none at all, or else is one way or another distorted.

A variety of personalities and minds, unresponsive to the action of grace, present an idea of Jesus in their own image and likeness. The world watches, and draws from the data at hand as accurate a conclusion as it can: for example, that religion makes people bow their neck, but not their will at its roots. This happens because some who call themselves disciples of Christ (but are still living in themselves, not Christ in them) cast the shadow of their own persons across the religion they profess. Consequently, and tragically, the separation goes on and is perpetuated, between those who are outside and those who ought to be attracting the world and drawing it to the Lord by reliving love which is God.

In other words, religion is disliked because it has been altered, whereas even the most agnostic people still feel a fascination, or at least respect however silent, for the missionary who ventures onto far coast lands, leaving everything for love of God, or for the martyr who consummates his life with his own blood.

And this, all of this, because either Christianity is genuine and fully lived or it is open to much criticism.

This all strikes the eye immediately in many cases. But on a higher, more subtle level, when we approach people who have given themselves to God heart and soul, it is not uncommon to detect disagreeable mistakes, even if in practice only, which obscure the beauty of our faith.

Some people's journey on our planet is so hard, this valley so full of tears, that the only comfort they find is in the cross; they grab hold of it and make it their personal banner; they present it to others also, teaching them to love it, but . . . they stop there. They stop there because, although they do truly love with all their heart, and concretely too, they have not enough faith in God's care for them and for everyone.

The paschal mystery stands to attest that Jesus is life which conquers death, he is light that floods the darkness, he is fullness that fills the void.

In the final analysis, this is Christianity. The cross is essential to it, as a means; tears are forerunners of consolation, and poverty of possession of the kingdom; purity draws back the curtain on heaven, persecution and meekness are preludes to the conquest of eternity and guarantee the Church's growth in the world.

On the fifteen mysteries which bejewel the full rosary, the Church assigns five which are joyful, five sorrowful, and five glorious. This means that it is always fitting for a Christian to hope, and to sing as the early Christians on the threshold of martyrdom, because we are the heirs of that fullness of joy which Jesus promised to and invoked upon everybody that would follow him.

Let us help each other to be in the Church—in our own small way—complete witnesses of that Jesus who drew our hearts. In this way we too can cooperate in making the Church more beautiful, and thus recognizable to all.

False Prudence

.

What ruins some souls is a false "prudence." They call it prudence, but it's a human prudence, and it springs up every time the divine surfaces. It has the appearance of virtue but is more aggravating than vice. It does not want to shake anyone up. It lets the rich go to hell ("you already have your reward," cf. Lk 6:24) by not enlightening them. Who knows what might happen? It lets the neighbors beat each other up, and even kill, because someone might accuse you of meddling in other people's affairs. You could even end up as a witness in a trial. Why bother to get involved? It advises moderation to the saints, lest something happen to them.

It isolates us. This prudence cuts us off, clamping us in like a vice, because it's born of fear.

It's especially scared of God. If he were to become too active in the world, through his faithful children, God could incite revolution; and those children's lives could be ruined, like Christ's; they could end up hated by the world, as he was.

It's a counterfeit virtue. I think it's planted or fertilized by the devil. He can do a lot of business in that climate. There once lived a man who had none of it. That was Christ Jesus. When he went out to preach, at the first lesson they wanted to kill him, there and then. "But he went straight through their midst and walked away" (Lk 4:30).

Look at his life with the eyes of this sort of prudent person and you would call the whole thing an imprudence. Not just that: If these prudent persons were logical in their reasoning, they would draw the conclusion that his death, his crucifixion . . . he asked for it . . . with his imprudence.

I don't believe there's a word spoken by Jesus that does not jar against these people. That is because God and the world are a complete antithesis. Only those who are able to emerge from the world to follow in the footsteps of Christ can make humanity hope for anything.

They Cannot Pass Through

"It is easier for a camel to pass through a needle's eye than for a rich man to enter the kingdom of God" (Mt 19:24). Any wealthy person who does not behave in accordance with Jesus' will is risking his eternity. But we are all rich, so long as Jesus is not yet fully alive in us.

Even the beggar, carrying a brown bag with nothing but a sandwich in it and cursing anyone who touches it, is no less rich than any other. His heart is set on something which is not God; unless he makes himself poor, in the gospel sense, he will not pass through into the kingdom of heaven.

The road to get there is a narrow one; only nothingness gets through. There are people who are rich in education, and their swollen-headedness blocks their way into the kingdom and the kingdom's entrance into them; the spirit of divine wisdom finds no room in their soul.

Another is rich in haughty conceit, another in human affections; so long as they do not break with all that, they are not with God. Everything must be excised from the heart and replaced with God, and with others in their God-given order of importance. There are people who own a wealth of worries; they don't know how to get rid of them by casting them into God's care. They live tortured lives. The joy and peace and charity of the kingdom of heaven are not theirs.

They cannot pass through.

Others' riches are their sins; they torment themselves by weeping over them, instead of incinerating them in the mercy of God and looking ahead, loving God and neighbor to make up for the times when they have not loved.

The
Secret
of
Love

Be On Guard

B e on guard . . ." (Lk 12:40). The gospel tells us to be on guard with belts fastened and lamps burning ready It promises that the master who finds the servant vigilant when he comes home will put on an apron and wait upon him.

Only love stays awake. Staying awake is characteristic of love. When you love someone your heart stays awake all the time, waiting for that person; every minute that passes is spent for that person's sake, watching and waiting. Jesus wants us to love. That is why he asks us to be wide-awake.

A frightened person too is on guard. In fact, Jesus says something about thieves. . . . You watch because you are afraid, and you are afraid because you love something you do not want to lose.

Jesus demands love. But for the sake of our salvation, since he loves us, he stimulates fear. He loves us like a mother who promises her children, depending on how they behave, either rewards or punishments.

Jesus is asking for nothing less than the pure love which gives itself without a thought for rewards. In the hope of seeing us safe, he shows us also rewards and punishments.

The Wise and Foolish Virgins

Wise virgins and foolish virgins (cf. Mt 25:1-13). The oil stands for love.

A person who possesses love is a virgin; consequently—from Christ's point of view—Mary Magdalen is more like a virgin than a lot of virgins proud of their virginity, or who, in any case, do not love.

And Jesus cannot recognize them, because love recognizes nothing but love. The bridegroom recognizes his spouse as the one who bears his surname, something of his own, almost his own self passed on to her and at one with him.

Properly speaking, God is charity, nothing characterizes him more than this; it is his very essence.

Though We Had Known God

After having come to know God, whenever we lack vigilance and let ourselves be crushed by the cross without capitalizing on the graces that come through it, our soul gropes in darkness and anguish. Having lost the merit of his light we search for him.

We search for love, calling for it, invoking it, crying out at times and groaning. But we do not find it. We do not find it because we do not love.

The Lord is unyielding. He has an immutable law. Heaven and earth will pass away (cf. Mk 13:31)—his own words know no exceptions.

The soul has no right to feel loved before she loves. She receives love when she has love. The Lord made her in his own image and likeness. He respects in her the dignity with which he invested her.

The soul has to take the initiative and be as it were the first to love, by responding to grace. Then God comes. He manifests himself to the one who loves him. He gives to one who has, and such a one will retain this love in plenty.

The soul that loves participates in the life of God and feels like she is in charge. She fears nothing. Everything for her acquires a new value.

We pass from death to life when we love.

Often Love Is Not Love

Since what is called love in the world is very frequently not really love, it has earned the saying that "love is blind." But when a soul applies itself to loving as God teaches—God who *is* love—she will very soon discover that love is a light. Besides, Jesus said it: "Whoever loves me . . . I too will love him and will manifest myself to him" (Jn 14:21).

A tornado of voices from all around frequently sweeps across our soul, especially when we have not yet learned what it is to love God. These are soundless voices, but strong: voices in the heart, voices of the intellect, voices of remorse and regret, voices of passion. . . . We follow now one, now another, doing all day what is dictated by these voices, or at least determined by them in some way.

That is why, though we are living in God's grace, our lives sometimes enjoy only brief patches of sunlight. The rest of life is sunk in a tedium frequently condemned by a voice stronger than all the others, as though to say that this is not true life, it is not life in its fullness.

If instead the soul turns to God and applies herself to loving him, and her love is true and concrete at every single moment, then from time to time she will notice that one voice will stand out among the many. This one is more of a light than a voice. It is like a tune which gently winds its way into the complicated concert of the soul. It is a thought, almost imperceptible, which offers itself to the soul, perhaps more delicate than the others, or more subtle. Sometimes this is the voice of God.

The soul then that has made a decision for God and has given everything to him, catches, from the swamp of voices surrounding it, a sparkle of clear limpid water. It is like finding a sapphire among the rocks, a nugget of gold in the sand.

The soul takes this gem, dusts it off, sets it in the light, and translates it into life.

Perhaps this soul has decided to journey to God together with others so that the Father may enjoy the sight of his children loving one another. After consulting with whoever represents God for her here on earth, she will communicate her treasure discreetly to others. Thus the wealth can be shared, the divine may circulate, and as in a competition we may learn from each other how to love God better. By doing this, the soul has doubly loved. She has loved by carrying out the will of God, and also by communicating with her neighbor. God, faithful to his eternal promises, will continue, step by step, to manifest himself to her.

How much this is to be desired! That our heart be immersed all day long in nothing but thoughts of heaven! That such thoughts fill us and overflow till our life, nourished by the sacraments, is deified!

We can give God to others if we have him already. We have him, if we love him.

Then we will be able to light up small suns in a dark and dull world, suns that will point out the way for many, suns that provide warmth in the total humility of their lives, lives completely sacrificed to the Lord, where they no longer speak for he speaks, where they live no more but he lives.

God Is Mighty, the Almighty

God is mighty. He is the almighty. Mary has been described as "almighty in grace." She too is powerful: Everything is possible for her, and her requests are always answered. We instead are greatly limited. And those among us who would think of themselves differently, are for that very reason one of us.

However, if we love God, then our powerlessness and our poverty might be to our advantage. It can help us obtain something.

Our Father in heaven wished Jesus to become our brother, and to prepare for his coming he made one human being immaculate, all because we are in a sorry state, spiritually wounded, sinners.

Sin is something we have to detest, but thinking of Jesus' arrival on earth through Mary can make us die for sheer joy unless we are upheld by God.

Jesus on earth . . . a brother to us who says: "If you ask the Father for something in my name, he will give it to you" (Mt 18:19; Jn 14:13-14). It's as if the good boy in the family, feeling sorry for his difficult brother, were to tell him, "Go to Dad and ask him for this in my name," confident of getting better results.

Jesus on earth . . . Jesus our brother . . . Jesus who dies between thieves for our sakes: the Son of God, treated just like anyone else.

Perhaps we ourselves have some influence on the Father's heart when we present ourselves as we are, wretched creatures, who have committed perhaps every sin in the book, but we're sorry and turn to his love, saying, "After all, if you came to us, it was our weakness that drew you, you were wounded with compassion for our sorry state."

There is certainly no mother or father on earth, looking for a wayward child and doing all they can to get him back, quite like our Father in heaven.

On Earth
As It Is
in Heaven

Not Mine But Yours

Not my will but yours be done" (Lk 22:42). Try hard to remain in his will and to keep his will abiding in you. When God's will is done on earth as it is in heaven, Jesus' last will and testament will be fulfilled.

Think of the sun and its rays. Take the sun as a symbol of the will of God, which is God himself. Imagine the rays symbolize God's will for each individual. Walk to the sun in the light of your own ray, diverse and distinct from everyone else's, and fulfill the marvelous design God has for you.

There's an unlimited number of rays, all pouring from the same sun . . . each a single will, special for each of us.

The closer the rays get to the sun, the closer they get to each other. We too, the closer we get to God, by doing his will more and more perfectly, the closer we get to each other.

Until we shall all be one.

Only One Will Is Good

Generally Christians use the expression "God's will be done" at sad moments, when all human avenues of help seem blocked. When a person faces the inevitable shattering of plans, hopes, and desires, then faith surfaces, and we accept with resignation what God has decreed. But this is not the only time when God's will should be done. There is more to Christianity than only this "Christian resignation."

A Christian's life is rooted in heaven as well as on earth. Through faith Christians can be, and always ought to be, in touch with an Other who is familiar with their lives and destinies. This Other is not earthly. No, he belongs to another world. Neither is he a merciless judge nor an absolute sovereign who asks only to be served. He is a Father because of his relationship with us, his children adopted through his only-begotten Son, who dwells with him from all eternity.

A Christian cannot determine his or her life by foresight and personal choice alone. How sad that so many people daily awake to expected boredom! They grumble over many things past, present, and to come, because they are the ones to create their own life's plan. But anything born of human intelligence and limited foresight cannot satisfy us completely, since we all hunger for the infinite. These people take the part of God, at least for what concerns their own lives; like the prodigal son they take their share and squander it as they please, without any regard to their father's advice.

So often we Christians are blind and renounce our supernatural dignity. Yes, we repeat every day in the Our Father, "Thy will be done on earth, as it is in heaven." But we neither understand what we're saying nor behave in conformity with what we pray for.

God is totally aware of the road we should take at every step of our lives. For each of us he has fixed a celestial orbit for the star of our freedom to travel. But we must abandon ourselves to him, our creator. We have our own orbit, our own life, that does not conflict with the orbits plotted for billions of others, offspring of the same Father as we. Ours harmonizes with theirs in a firmament more splendid than that of the stars, because it is spiritual. God must manage our life and guide it into the divine adventure we cannot foresee, but where we offer the contribution of our free will from moment to moment, at once spectators and protagonists, in wonderful scenarios of love.

We *can* offer our will, freely and lovingly. Not, we ought to offer it or, what is worse, resign ourselves to offering it.

God is a Father, and therefore he is love. He is the creator, our redeemer, and our sanctifier. Who better than he knows what is good for us?

"Lord, let it be done. Yes. Let your divine will be done now and at all times. May it be done with me, with my children, with others, with their children too, and with all humanity.

"Be patient, Lord, and pardon us. We are blind. Pardon us for not understanding. We have shut our eyes and declared by the lives we lead that all is darkness and heaven does not exist. And thus we have forced heaven to remain closed. By our blindness, we have prevented heaven from bequeathing its gifts to earth.

"Draw us into the rays of your light, of our light. Draw us into the ray that your love determined when out of love you gave us being.

"Every moment thrust us onto our knees in adoration of your will: the only will that is good, delightful, holy, new, rich, fascinating, fertile. Thus, when the hour of sorrow arrives, we may be capable of seeing your infinite love beyond the trial. Then we may be so filled with you that, while still on earth, we can see with your eyes. We may observe from on high the divine tapestry woven by you for us and for our neighbor. In this God-woven fabric everything turns out to be a brilliant web of love. Spare us, at least a little, the sight of those knots which your loving-kindness, seasoned with justice, has tied in the places where our blindness broke the thread of your will.

"May your will be done throughout the world, then a secure peace will descend to earth, for the angels told us so: 'Peace on earth to those on whom his favor rests' (Lk 2:14). And if you, Christ, have told us that only one is good, the Father, then in consequence only one will is good, your Father's will."

Heaven and Earth Will Pass Away

I am becoming increasingly aware that "heaven and earth will pass away . . ." (Mk 13:31), but God's plan for us will not pass away. Complete satisfaction comes only from finding ourselves always in the space which God has intended for us from all eternity.

I Was Hungry
and
You Gave Me to Eat

Great God, through Jesus Christ you have revealed
Yourself to be a God of compassion for those who suffer.

A Prayer in Time of Suffering

Until my healing comes, Lord, give me Your grace so that I may accept my suffering. Give me Your strength so that I will not despair. Give me Your love so that my suffering may bring me closer to You, the origin and source of all love.

Amen.

Give Me All the Lonely People

L ord, give me all those lonely people . . . My heart has felt the passionate desire which invades yours over the abandoned state in which the whole world is afloat.

I feel love for each one who is sick and alone. Whom do they have to comfort their tears? Who shows compassion for them
    in their slow death?
Who hugs to their own heart
    the heart in despair?
O my God, grant that I may be in the world a tangible sacrament of your love; let me be your arms, hugging to myself all the loneliness in the world and consuming it with love.

The Exam

If you were a student and happened to learn what questions were going to be on the final exam, you would consider yourself very fortunate and study the answers from first to last.

Life is a test. At its end we too must pass an exam: But God's infinite love has already told us the questions: "I was hungry and you gave me to eat, I was thirsty and you gave me to drink" (Mt 25:35). The works of mercy will be the subject of examination through which God can tell whether or not we have really loved him by serving him in our neighbor. This is perhaps the reason why the pope often simplifies the Christian life for us by underlining these works of mercy.

We do the will of Jesus in heaven by transforming our lives into a continual work of mercy.

Fundamentally it is not difficult; it does not make many changes in what we already do. It is a question of placing every relationship with our neighbor onto a supernatural level. Whatever our calling may be, as mothers or fathers, farmers or office workers, congressional leaders or heads of state, students or laborers—during the day there are continual opportunities, direct or indirect, for giving food to the hungry, instructing the ignorant, putting up with tiresome people, counseling the confused (or doubtful), and praying for the living and the dead.

This gives a new purpose to every action in favor of our neighbors, whoever they may happen to be, and every day of our lives will help us to be ready for the eternal day, as we pile up goods which the moth cannot consume.

Expanding One's Heart

O ur heart must expand to the greatness of the heart of Jesus. What a task! But it is the one thing necessary. If this is done, all is done. It is a matter of loving everyone around us as God loves them. Given that we are living in time, we love our neighbors one at a time, not holding on to traces of affection for the person we met a minute ago. After all, in each we love the same Jesus. But when that trace of the other remains, it means that the person was loved for our own sake or for theirs . . . not for Jesus. This is the difficulty.

The most important thing for us is preserving divine chastity, to keep the kind of love in our hearts that Jesus has. This does not mean that in order to be pure we need to deprive our heart and repress its power to love. Instead, make it as big as the heart of Jesus and love all people. Isn't just one consecrated host, from among the millions of hosts on earth, sufficient to nourish oneself with God? Just one neighbor—the one God's will has placed beside us—is sufficient to give us communion with all of humanity, which is the mystical Christ.

Furthermore, communion with our neighbor is the second commandment, the one which follows directly from the love of God as a way of giving it expression.

Being Love

Some people do things out of love. Others do them trying to "*be* love." Those who do things "out of love" may do good, perhaps thinking they are doing their neighbor a great service. If he is sick, they may bore him with their talk, with their advice, or with their help; with a charity that is not very sensitive, but even tiresome.

Poor people! They'll not be without merit, but to their neighbor they'll be a burden, all because one needs to "*be* love."

Our destiny is like that of the planets. They exist if they revolve; if they don't revolve they don't exist. We exist—I am not referring to our own life, but to God's life in us—if we don't stop loving for a moment.

Love settles us in God. God is Love.

But the kind of love that God is, is light. In that light we can see whether our way of approaching our neighbors and serving them is consistent with the heart of God, with the way they would like or imagine it if they had not us but Jesus beside them.

Mercy Over Sacrifice

When one has known pain in all its cruel nuances, in its various forms of anguish, and has reached out to God in agonized, speechless supplication, in meek cries for help; when one has drained the chalice to its dregs, for days or years offering one's own cross to God, fused with his (which gives ours divine value), then comes the time when God takes pity on us and takes us into union with him.

At this moment, when the unique value of pain has been learned by experience, and one has come to believe in the economy of the cross, having seen its beneficent effects, the Lord reveals in a new and higher form something worth even more than pain. This is love of our neighbor in the shape of mercy, the kind of love which opens our heart and arms to the wretched, the needy, to those who have been broken by life, to the repentant sinners.

The sort of love that can take in all who have lost their way, be they friend, brother or sister, or stranger, and never stops forgiving. Love which celebrates the return of a sinner more than it does a thousand righteous, lending to God our intelligence and the goods necessary to be able to show joy to the prodigal son at his return.

A love that doesn't measure and will not be measured.

This is charity grown more abundant, more universal, and more concrete than what the soul had before. It even feels the rise of sentiments resembling those of Jesus; it notices divine words surfacing on its own lips for whomever it meets: "My heart is moved with pity for the crowd" (Mt 15:32). Mercy is the ultimate expression of charity, what caps it off. Charity surpasses pain, which belongs only to this life, whereas love carries on into the next. The Lord prefers mercy to sacrifice.

In Love, What Matters Is Loving

In love, what matters is loving. That's how it is on this earth. Love—I am speaking of supernatural love, which does not exclude what is natural—is so simple, but so complex. You have to do your part, and the others theirs.

If you try to live out of love, you will find that on this earth it's best to do your part. You never know if you will receive the other's response; you do not need to. You will be disappointed sometimes, but you will never lose heart if you convince yourself that in love, what counts is just loving.

Love Jesus in your neighbor, Jesus who always returns your love, though perhaps through other means.

Indeed, he gives you a soul of steel to face the storms, yet softens your soul with love toward everyone around you—provided that you keep in mind that in love, what matters is loving.

The
Greatest
Treasure

If We Are United,
Jesus Is Present among Us

If we are united, Jesus is here. This is of great value, worth more than every other treasure our heart can possess. It's worth more than having a mother, a father, brothers and sisters, or children. It is worth more than a home, than work, than property; worth more than the art treasures of a city like Rome, worth more than our business, than natural surroundings with their flowers and meadows, than the sea and the stars; more than the life of our soul.

He is the one who gave every era its name by inspiring the saints of the time with his eternal truths.

Ours too is his hour: not so much the hour of a particular saint, but his, of him present among us, living in our midst—building his mystical body through the unity of love.

But we have to spread Christ; make him increase in other members; become bearers of fire, like him.

Make all into one, and bring the One into everybody!

And therefore, let us live the life which he gives us, from moment to moment, in charity.

Reciprocal love is the basic commandment. As a result, everything built on it has value. There is no value in what we do if it is not done with the sentiment of love for our neighbor—because the Lord is our Father, and he always has only his children at heart.

To Live Life Fully

Christians are called to live their lives fully, to swim in the light, to plunge into a sea of crosses, and not to mope. Instead, all too frequently our life is listless, our mind is misty, our will indecisive. Why? Because educated in the ways of the world, we have become used to living as individuals. This is a contradiction of the Christian life.

Christ is love. The Christian cannot be anything else. Love generates communion. Communion is the foundation and the summit of the Christian life. In this life of communion people go to God no longer by themselves; they journey together. This is a reality of incomparable beauty, which reminds us of a verse of Holy Scripture: "Behold how good and how pleasant it is for brethren to dwell together in unity!" (Ps 133:1).

However, fraternal communion is not a static beatitude. It requires repeated conquests. It results not only in maintaining communion continually, but also in making it overflow to many, because the communion we are talking about is love, charity. And charity of its nature spreads itself to others.

How often unity weakens among those who have chosen to go to God together because dust infiltrates and clogs their relationships. The charm is lost. The light that came on between them slowly fades out. This "dust" may be a worry, an attachment of the heart to oneself or to others, a loving of self for self's sake and not for God, or of our neighbor or neighbors for themselves instead of for God. At other times it may be a backing off of the heart that had previously given itself to others, a concentration on one's self, one's own will, instead of focusing on God, or upon one's neighbor for God, or on God's will.

Very often it is a false judgment about those with whom we live. Once we said that we chose to see only Jesus in our neighbors, to relate to Jesus in our neighbors, and to love Jesus in them.

But then we begin to remember that this neighbor has this or that defect, he or she is imperfect in one way or another.

We lose our simple way of viewing others.

We are no longer lit up from within. As a result, unity gets broken through our own fault.

Perhaps that neighbor has made mistakes. All of us have. But how does God see him now? What is his real condition, the truth about his situation? If he has put himself right with God, God no longer remembers what he did, he has erased the whole thing with his own blood. So why should I remember? Who is in the wrong now?

I who judge, or my neighbor?

I am.

So I have got to apply myself to seeing things as God sees them, in the light of truth, and treat my neighbors accordingly, so that if, unfortunately, they might not yet be reconciled with the Lord, the warmth of my love, which is Christ himself in me, may bring them to repent, the way the sun warms and heals our wounds.

Charity is maintained by truth, and the truth is pure mercy. From head to toe we must clothe ourselves with mercy if we want to call ourselves Christians.

Does my neighbor wish to return to unity with me?

Then I must see my neighbor afresh as if nothing had happened. I must start life together as at the beginning, in the unity of Christ, because nothing now stands between us. Such trust will safeguard my neighbor from falling again. If I have this measure with my neighbor, I too may hope to be judged by God one day in the same manner.

The Words of a Father

The words of a father are always worth a lot, because one must trust a person who speaks out of love. But when a father speaks his last words, before leaving this earth, those words are chiseled into his children's minds and worth as much as all the rest put together: They are his testament.

Compared to God's love, a father's love is nothing. Jesus, God become human, spoke too. He too left a testament: "That they may be one . . . that all may be one" (Jn 17:11,21).

Whoever makes unity the goal of life has struck the center of God's heart.

We are all brothers and sisters in this world, but we pass each other by, ignoring one another. This can happen even between baptized Christians.

We have the communion of saints and the Mystical Body. Yet this body is like a network of unlit tunnels.

We have the power to light them: in many, grace is a living presence. But that is not all that Jesus was after when he turned to invoke his Father. He wanted a heaven on earth: The union of all with God and with each other, lighting up the tunnels with the presence of Jesus not only within each soul but also within every relationship.

This was his testament, the supreme desire of the God who gave his life for us.

I Was Sick

I saw someone in a hospital ward, all incased in plaster. Thorax and arm, the right arm, were, as it were, locked up. He managed everything with his left hand, the best he could. The plaster was torment, but his left arm, even if more tired come evening, was growing stronger, doing the work of two.

We are members of one another, mutual service is an obligation. Jesus did not just advise this, he gave it as a command.

Let us not think that we are being saints, if we are serving somebody out of charity. If our neighbor is disabled, we must help him out, giving him the help he would give himself if he were able. Otherwise, just what sort of Christians are we?

At the last judgment, we shall hear this repeated by Jesus: "I was sick . . . and you visited me" (Mt 25:36). I was imprisoned, I was naked, I was hungry . . . Jesus likes to hide precisely in the suffering and the deprived.

Then, when our own time comes and we need our neighbor's charity, let's not feel humiliated. Let us even then be aware of our own dignity, and with all our heart thank whoever is helping us, reserving the greatest thanks of all for God, who has made the human heart charitable, and for Christ. By announcing the Good News with his own blood, especially his new commandment, he has stimulated countless souls to help one another.

If we Christians do not manifest this distinguishing sign, we become indistinguishable from the world. We no longer deserve to be called "children of God." Foolishly we neglect to use the most powerful weapon for giving evidence of God in this atmosphere frozen by atheism, which has become pagan, indifferent and superstitious. Would that the world could watch with amazement a spectacle of a people united, and say of us as of our glorious predecessors: "See how they love one another."

Jesus
Crucified
and
Forsaken

The Cross

"Let him take up his cross . . ." (Mt 16:24). What a strange and singular expression! But, like the other sayings of Jesus, even this one glimmers with that light that the world does not know. It shines so brightly that weak human eyes, belonging to lukewarm Christians too, are dazzled by it and blinded.

There may be nothing more puzzling than the cross, or more difficult to grasp; it does not penetrate the human brain or heart. It does not find its way in, because it is not appreciated, the reason being that too many of us have become only nominal Christians; baptized yes, practicing perhaps, but immensely far off from what Jesus wishes us to be.

We hear about the cross in Lent, we kiss it on Good Friday; we put it up on the wall. The sign of the cross is used over some things we do, but who understands it? Isn't the root of the problem our misunderstanding of the word "love"?

"Love" is the most beautiful but the most distorted, the most debased of the words we use. It stands for the essence of God, the life of God's children; the Christian breathes it, but it has been taken over and monopolized by the world; it is a word misused by people who really have no right to mention it.

Sure enough, it is not so with every kind of love in the world: maternal feeling, for instance, ennobles love because it involves pain. There is brotherly love, married love, filial love, which are healthy and good, traces (unconsciously maybe) of the love of the Father, the Creator of all.

But the supreme love is what does not get understood: the fact that God who made us descended to us as a man among others, lived with us, stayed with us and let himself be nailed on the cross for us—all for our salvation.

This is too much, too beautiful, too divine, too unlike what is human, too bloody, painful and extreme to grasp.

One might get some idea of it through maternal love. A mother's love is made up of more than kisses and caresses; above all it means sacrifice.

So too with Jesus: Love drove him to the cross, which most people think was crazy.

But only that folly saved humanity and fashioned saints.

In fact, the saints are the ones capable of understanding the cross. By following Jesus, the God-man, they picked up their daily cross as the most precious thing they could find; sometimes they brandished it like a weapon when they became soldiers of God; they loved it all their life long and experienced what they already knew: That the cross is *the key*, the only one that opens up a treasure, *the* treasure. Bit by bit it opens souls to communion with God. Thus through people God reappears on earth and repeats—of course in an immensely inferior way, but similarly—what he once did as a man amongst the people of his time, as he blessed those who cursed him, pardoned those who insulted him, saved, cured, gave heavenly directives, satisfied the hungry, founded a new society upon love, displayed the dynamism of the One who sent him. So the cross is the indispensable instrument to make what is divine pierce what is human, enabling us to share more fully in the life of God and be raised from the realms of this world to the kingdom of heaven.

But you have to "take up your own cross," wake up in the morning looking forward to it, knowing those gifts the world does not know can come to us no other way: such peace and joy, such knowledge of celestial things, beyond the experience of the great majority.

The cross . . . such a familiar thing. So dependable, it never fails to show up for its daily appointment. We could become saints if we only welcomed it.

The cross is the emblem of the Christian. The world wants no part of it, believing that to escape from it is to escape pain, not realizing how, to those who appreciate it, it opens the soul to the kingdom of light and of love: that very love the world longs for, but lacks.

A Unique Strategy

I've noticed your strategy is consistent but never monotonous. Maybe it is because you *are* your own action. You are love that is always new. This is your strategy: When souls are satisfied with shadows (and I'm not speaking of mortal shadows, but when their life is lived for you but is not you), often you send pain. The soul then comes back and says its yes to you. There are times when that yes is fragranced with a feeling of profound gratitude and plunges into a singular prayer: "Yes Lord, when I meet your cross I find you on it. Thank you for calling me back to you yourself and not only to what are your concerns, because I am drawn to solitude with you more than to anything else, to the same solitude I shall be obliged to face anyway on the day when we meet if not chosen now with love.

"May you, who can do all things, procure for me in your name the grace to arrive at that continual conversation between you-in-me and you, where events, people, and things are nothing but fuel for our pure love."

This alone is true life, because it is a spark of yourself: a life without deception or disappointments, with no interruptions and no sunset.

His Mass and Ours

If you are suffering,
and your kind of suffering puts a halt to
 everything you might be doing,
think of the Mass.

In the Mass, today just like then,
Jesus is not working, neither is he preaching:
He is sacrificing himself out of love.
There are so many things that could be
 done in a lifetime,
so many things to say;
but however silent and inaudible to others,
the voice of pain,
offered for love,
speaks the loudest.
It pierces heaven.
If you are suffering,

plunge your pain into his:
Offer your own Mass,
and don't let it trouble you
    if the world does not understand.
It is enough that Jesus, Mary,
    and the saints understand you.
Live with them,
and shed your blood for the good
    of humanity, as he did.
The Mass!
It is beyond our understanding!
His Mass, and ours.

I Know Nothing but Christ
and Him Crucified

I have but one Spouse on earth:
Jesus crucified and forsaken;
apart from him I have no other God.
All of heaven is in him, with the Trinity;
all of earth, with the human race.
So I have all that is *his*, and nothing else.
All pain is *his*, and therefore mine.
I shall walk through the world,
looking for him every moment of my life.
What hurts me is *mine*.
Mine the pain affecting me now.
Mine the pain of souls beside me
(that is my Jesus).
Mine all that is not peace, joy, beauty,
        loveable or serene.

In one word: whatever is not heaven,
because I have my own heaven,
the one in my Spouse's heart.
I have no feeling for any others.
For the years that are left me
I will be thirsting for pain, anguish, despair,
    loss, exile, abandonment, agony—
for *everything* that is he who is pain.
So I will drink down the water of tribulation
from many hearts that are nearby,
and through communion with my
    almighty Spouse,
from many far away.
I'll pass through like fire
burning everything that needs
    to come down,
leaving only the truth standing.
I must be like him, or rather
be him in the present moment of my life.

The Cold

Cold freezes; but it can burn and cut if extreme. Wine fortifies us; but too much weakens our faculties. Motion is what it is, but when whirling fast it looks like it is standing still.

The Spirit of God is the giver of life, but a large dose of him intoxicates us.

Jesus is love because he is God; but the great love he had for us led him to cry out: "My God, my God, why have you forsaken me?" (Mt 27:46). At such a moment he appears to be merely human.

We Would Simply Die

We would simply die if we did not fix our gaze on you; as if magically, you transform every bitterness into sweetness: We see you brought to a complete standstill as you cry out from the cross in absolute inactivity, in a living death. You hurled all your fire upon the earth as you turned cold, and finishing your life there, you flung infinite, endless life into us, who live it now with elation.

We want nothing more than to see ourselves like you, at least a little, joining our pain to yours and offering it to the Father.

So that we might possess the light, you lost your sight.

To acquire union for us, you experienced separation from the Father.

So that we might have wisdom, you made yourself ignorance.

To clothe us in innocence, you became sin.

So that God might be present in us, you felt him far away from you.

I Would Like to Bear Witness

I would like to bear witness to the whole world that Jesus forsaken has filled every void, illumined all darkness, accompanied all loneliness, annulled every pain, wiped out every sin.

Whoever Does Not Renounce

"Ｎone of you can be my disciple if he does not renounce all his possessions" (Lk 14:33).

"None of you": So these words of Jesus are directed to every Christian.

"All his possessions." It's required of all people who want to be Christians. We cannot be attached even to our own soul (it is one of the things we own), we must be detached from everything.

Jesus crucified and forsaken is the universal teacher for this.

God's
Artwork

The Lives of Saints

There is something unique about the lives of saints, although there is great variety among them. After they give themselves to God, they are taken into his special care. As supreme Artist and supreme Love, he makes them into works of divine art. Angelic powers and the eyes of other saints are able to comprehend them, or else an intelligence illuminated by the singular grace given to persons commissioned by the Church to examine them. To the rest of us, for the most part, their interior life is invisible, incomprehensible, because it is God more than the human person who lives in the saint, and only the pure of heart can see God.

A saint's life is made up of deep valleys and high peaks: gaping chasms, nights as murky as

Hades, dismal tunnels, where a soul invaded by a totally superior light is dazzled in obscure contemplation and sunk in a sea of anguish close to desperation by the glaring realization of one's own nothingness and poverty. Saints spend months, even years, yearning for nothing but to die on the breast of God, from whom they sometimes feel irreparably separated. Life becomes an atrocious death, sleep a great relief soothing the soul's sores. They go through long periods when they cry out for forgiveness, for salvation, and there's nothing left in their heart but God, their own God.

Then, after a long period in a crucible—a sort of "purgatory"—the soul is drawn out by the celestial Artist into the light, slowly but surely adapting to a serene, full and active life—and able to survive all collisions without a scratch. But there lives now in them, no longer the self, but the creator and Lord of every human heart, glorious, strong, honored, and listened to.

At this time a strange and rare divine vigor rises in the saint's spirit, and produces opposite characteristics: strength and gentleness, justice and mercy, prudence and simplicity. They enjoy life in God, and offer their Master "sacrifices of joy" (cf. Ps 27:6), joy of a kind the world does not know. They cannot help thinking there is no dream to compare with such a fabulous life as they enjoy, harmonious and fruitful and so loving as to be divine. God employs them for the great works which adorn and build the heavenly city, his Church, predestined to return to God as a beautiful bride, worthy of Christ its founder.

We are given only one life; it would be appropriate to put it back into the hands of the one who gave it. This would be—for any person who is rational and free—the most intelligent thing to do; the way to maintain and extend one's own freedom and to correspond with the divine plan; it would mean the deifying of one's own poor existence in the name of him who said: "You are gods, all of you children of the Most High" (Ps 82:6).

The Saint's Masterpiece

O n entering the parlor of a convent of recent or ancient foundation, or its long corridors, one often finds an image of the founder on the wall, not rarely a saint, holding his or her Rule. Someone dropping in from outside may little understand the significance of this.

The majority of people, atheists too, feel the charm of a saint. But they like to imagine saints either in the ecstasies of contemplation, or mixing with the people they benefit, or doing those things which get passed on by word of mouth which nearly always surround the person of a saint: insignificant acts, at times, externalized by something that would have come from no one else but this saint who was guided by God, a saying or gesture in which the obvious and unmistakable mingling of the divine with the human is present, introducing a new note, revolutionary sometimes, into the boring, uneventful, everyday life of the world.

But a holy founder is not just that.

Founders are people who have fulfilled God's will. They have made every effort to be perfect as the Father is perfect, making the generous gift of their selves to God more and more complete.

In reality the saint is a little father or a little mother, for God is love. To be filled with God means becoming a sharer in Love's divine fertility.

One comes to understand founders very well by looking at their accomplishments.

The most important of the saints' good works is the flock which has followed them, whether numerous or not, that they have coordinated into a family by means of the gospel's eternal laws, to which they gave a powerful contemporary resonance through the working of the Holy Spirit in their own spirit: for them it represents what for a mother is her child.

When founders believe their work with God is completed, they abandon themselves to him like an instrument in the hands of an artist to hammer out the essential lines of their work by writing a rule. They have to do it and they want to do it, with the conviction of a mother who says, "This and no other is my child."

Her baby is the reward a mother receives for all her suffering. More than anything else of hers, it is a living reminder of her joys and of the love which tied her to its father. It has its own features, enjoys a character of its own and blood of its own.

The saints love God with a love as far above human love as the heavens from the earth, a love which is the occasion of small or immense pain for them, and of small or ineffable joy in the God of the beatitudes. The joys and pains are not ends in themselves. They are a means for the Church's acquisition of a new work from God, for which the Lord is designing definite features with unmistakable characteristics, into which he infuses divine blood, namely the special spirit that shapes it, whose benefit is needed by some of the human population in that era.

The rule defines and explains this new work, keeping it intact, and for this reason it is the saint's masterpiece.

Launched into Infinity

The saints are great people
who have seen their greatness
in the Lord,
and risked everything they had for him
whose children they are.
They give without asking.
They offer their life, their soul, their joy,
earthly ties and every talent.
Liberated and alone,
launched into infinity,
they await from Love
their introduction to the realms of eternity.
But, already in this world,
they feel their souls brimming with love,
with real love, the only love that satisfies,
that gives the comfort

that breaks through the soul's eyelids
with fresh tears.
Ha! Nobody knows who a saint is.
The saint gave and now receives.
And an uninterrupted flow
courses between heaven and earth,
connecting earth to heaven;
a celestial lymph, extraordinary elation,
falls from heaven,
not halting at the saint
but pouring over the weary, the dying,
over the spiritually blind and paralyzed,
it bursts through and refreshes,
attracts and restores, and saves.
If you want to know what love is,
ask someone who is holy.

How Can We Become Saints?

Souls are often attracted by the idea of sanctity. Maybe it is actually the grace of God at work, stirring up such a desire in them.

Thinking about the preciousness of saints, of the influence of their personalities on their times, of the widespread and ongoing revolution that they have contributed to the world, is often the way the fire of this longing gets kindled. But at times the soul so sweetly tormented by this idea looks to the saints as if confronted with an impassable mountain or an impenetrable wall.

"What could I do to become a saint?" the soul asks.

"What test, what system, what practices, what ways to follow are there?"

"If I knew that penance would do it, I would flagellate myself from dawn to dusk. If I knew that it takes prayer, I would pray night and day. If it were sufficient to be a preacher, I would love to go through the cities and villages, giving myself no rest to bring God's word to everybody . . . but I don't know, I simply don't know the way."

Every saint has features of his or her own, saints look as different from one another as the greatest variety of flowers in a garden. . . .

But maybe there is a way which is good for everyone.

Maybe we do not need to figure out our own way, nor draw up plans or dream up a program; instead, plunge ourselves into the fleeting moment to fulfill for that instant the wish of him who called himself "the Way" (Jn 14:6), the best of ways. The past moment exists no longer; the next shall perhaps never be ours. But it is certain that we can love God in the moment granted us at present. Holiness gets built in time.

Nobody knows their own holiness; often not another person's either, so long as we are alive. It is only when the soul has completed her course and taken her exam, that she reveals to the world what was God's plan for her.

Nothing remains for us but to build it from moment to moment, responding with all our heart, soul, and strength to the love God bears

us personally and totally as our heavenly Father
with the liberality of the charity of a God.

The Divine Game

If a soul gives itself to God sincerely, he works on it. Pain and love are the primary pieces used in this divine game. Pain to excavate great chasms in the soul; love as a pain reliever; and more love, to fill up the soul and grant it the equilibrium of peace. The soul is conscious of being protected beneath the mighty hand of God and, even through tears, stands in silent attention to its Beloved at work.

But there are moments when God works on a soul to a point where it gets crushed by greater agonies than death itself. It feels deprived of help, without spiritual support from anybody. The entire world turns into nothing but a limitless desert.

That is the moment for a new miracle: unqualified trust, with desperate confidence in God who allows her pains and her nights (to prepare her for heaven), which initiates a new conversation between her and God, perceptible to nobody else. "Lord," she says, "you can see the deadly darkness around me. You see the extreme quandary my spirit is in, and you know how no one seems able to calm me. Take me under your own care. I put my trust in you and work for you in the interests of heaven and the expectation of arriving at Life."

It is like the petals of a flower, unfolded to God's love; rising from the stalk toward the sun, closer and closer to its light and heat. On and on, until the moment determined by God for it to become fused with him, no longer vacillating, no longer alone, but finally at peace forever, in God, the infinite sea of peace.

Mother
of Each
and
Every One

Coming to Know Mary

People do not easily understand Mary, yet they greatly love her. Even in a heart which is far from God, it is easier to find devotion to her than devotion to Jesus.

She is universally loved for the simple reason that she is a mother.

In general, mothers are not "understood." They are simply loved, especially by little children. It often happens that even an eighty-year-old will die, uttering as his last word "Mother."

Mothers are more the object of feeling than of thought. They inspire more poetry than philosophy, because they are something too deep and too real, too close to the human heart.

So it is with Mary, the mother of all mothers. The sum of all the affection, goodness, and kindness in all the world's mothers cannot equal hers.

Jesus sort of stands in front of us. His splendid, divine words differ too much from ours to be confused with them. What's more, they are a sign of contradiction.

Mary is as peaceful as nature, pure, calm, clear, moderate, beautiful. We might compare her to the wonders of nature far removed from the world: the mountains, the countryside, the sea, the clear blue or starry sky. She is like nature— strong, vigorous, orderly, reliable, firm, rich in hope, for year after year nature's life beneficently returns dressed in the transient beauty of flowers, charitable with its wealth of fruit.

Mary is too simple and too close to us to be "contemplated."

She is sung by hearts which are pure and in love with her. This is how such hearts give expression to the best in themselves. She brings the divine gently to earth, like an inclined plane from heaven, which descends from the sky's dizzy heights to the infinite smallness of God's creatures. She is Mother of each and every one. She alone knows the "baby-talk" to use with her infant, the unique way to smile and chuckle so that, however small each person is, they can now enjoy her caress and respond to that love with their own.

Mary is too close to us for us to be able to understand her. Chosen by the eternal Father to bring to us the graces, the divine gems of his Son, she is here beside us, always waiting in the hope that we will notice her and accept her gift.

And when persons find the fortune of understanding her, she steals them into her kingdom of peace, where Jesus is king and the Holy Spirit the breath of that heaven.

There, our souls purified and our darkness alight, we will contemplate her and rejoice in her as though she were an added heaven, a heaven apart.

Here, let us merit her calling us to "her way," not in remaining spiritually small where our love becomes only supplications, implorations, requests and interests, but in coming to know her, to give glory to her through our lives.

The Loveliness of Our Mother

How lovely our mother is in that perpetual recollection which the gospel attributes to her: "She kept all these words in her heart" (Lk 2:51).

That complete silence holds a fascination for souls who love.

Is there some way even I could live Mary's mystical silence, though it's our vocation to talk sometimes to evangelize, risking it in all kinds of places, rich or poor, in workshops, or out on the street, in schools, everywhere?

Our mother also spoke. She gave Jesus to us. The world has seen no greater apostle. No one ever had as much to say as she who gave *the Word*.

Our mother truly deserved the title, "Queen of Apostles," although she kept silent; silent because she and Jesus could not both speak at once. Speech must always rest upon silence, as a painting needs a background.

She was silent because she is a creature. Nothingness is unable to speak. Jesus spoke in the silence of that nothingness, uttering himself.

The Lord, the creator and all, spoke with the nothingness of his creature as a background.

Can one "live Mary"? How can my life acquire the fragrance of her charm? By quieting the creature within me, letting the Spirit of the Lord speak in this silence.

This is a way I can live both Mary and Jesus. I'll live Jesus within Mary. I am living Jesus by living Mary.

I Want to See Her Again in You

I entered a church one day.
With a heart full of trust, I asked him:
"Why did you choose to remain on earth,
everywhere on earth,
in the sweet eucharist,
yet despite being God
you did not find a way
to leave Mary with us as well,
a mother to us all on this journey?"
Out of the silence, he seemed to answer:
"I did not do so,
because I want to see her again in you.
Even though you are not immaculate,
my love will 'virginize' you.
And you, all of you,
will open your maternal hearts and arms

he who follows
me will not walk
in darkness but
will have the

light of life

John 8, 12

to humanity,
which now, as then, is thirsting for its God,
and for God's mother too.
Now it is up to you
to soothe the pains, the wounds,
to dry the tears.
Sing the litanies,
and try to see your own reflection in them."

Today's Virgins

In the field of technology, in fact in every field of human life, our modern age has witnessed many discoveries, innovations and newly-created needs. It also offers new forms of religious life. Phenomena unthought of not long ago take their place alongside others which have weathered the centuries but remain contemporary.

Through the Secular Institutes, for instance, the life of perfection and consecration to God is brought out of monasteries and convents, God's fortresses of yesterday and today, and infiltrates the whole world. This represents some progress. It is a sign of a certain maturation. On the one hand it shows God's love for humanity, which is always thirsty for what is pure and divine, a humanity which the virgin is destined to serve. On the other hand it reveals an increase in our

Lord's trust in his creatures, despite the treacherous heresies of our century. God fortifies his confidence, of course, with the graces he gives, corresponding to the virgins' needs.

The virgin, the woman consecrated to God, faces danger in today's world: in offices, in schools, on the subway, in lunchrooms. And despite the vulnerability of her sex, she is no longer shielded by a veil, nor by the walls of a convent and its grille. Neither has she the community schedule regulating her life with its checks and helps, nor the ever vigilant eye of a superior.

Fewer externals as an aid to her donation and her promise require a greater internal charge of energy. Without it she cannot keep herself detached from the world where she lives, and hold on faithfully to her union with him who chose her, who in fact selected her as his bride—he whose nature is incompatible with the spirit of this world.

Naturally she is deprived of the enchanting atmosphere of the cloister. Its silence and enclosure might have brought home more vividly the meaning of her gift of self. But still, an incomparable reality comforts her, a stimulus and an example, with a guiding star, incomparably brighter than any other flame: the Virgin of virgins. In beauty and dignity, in sanctity and in grace she not only surpasses all people, but all angels. Both acclaim her as their Queen.

Mary lived with people in the midst of the world. Nevertheless there never has been, nor ever will be, any created being more united to the Lord than she. She can tell today's virgins the secret of perfection, how we can climb to God though surrounded by the stunning noise of the world.

Mary has her own way, as both virgin and mother. She is her Son's mother. Through him she is the mother of all humanity. This virgin's convent spreads over the whole world. Mary is like a public fountain where everybody can drink. She is filled with maternal love for souls, a clean, bright, living reflection of the love that is God. She is almost the embodiment of love, the arms, as it were, of heaven's providence stretched out to humanity, to dry its tears, close its wounds, and point toward eternity.

The Virgin Mary did not wear any special dress. She wore the clothes of her time. Consequently when today's virgin thinks of Mary, she does not feel she is failing in any way by dressing like other women. Indeed her clothes become dear to her, clothes that she adapts as well as she can to the fashion of her day. She no longer likes the fashion for itself but for others' sake. Such clothing permits her heart on fire with the love of God access to the hearts of others who do not know him. Clothing can be an asset to her mission, part of the armory she employs in battling for the Lord. She cherishes the means because the end is the best there can be.

The Virgin Mary did not have other virgins as companions to meet with all the time. She was alone with God: with God before the incarnation, with God her Son after his nativity, with God in heaven after his ascension.

Her solitude did not deprive her of contemplation. On the contrary, it is natural for solitude to favor mystical union with the Lord.

Today's virgins, whom God has scattered across this world's darkness like small stars in the blackness of the firmament, are also solitary.

They are not solitary because others do not love them. We meet in them very often a verification of the scripture saying: "More numerous are the children of the deserted . . . than the children of her who has a husband" (Is 54:1).

They are only solitary because, as Jesus himself said of the state of virginity: "Not everyone can accept this teaching" (Mt 19:11). Virgins, precisely in their most beautiful and sacred gift, are misunderstood by the world, and at times even despised. In this they find that food of blood and tears that can make their spiritual maternity fertile, and they secure their guarantee to work for the Eternal, for him who died on the cross a virgin, drawing all the world to himself.

The solitude of the virgin in the world is appealing. Being alone she is united to God and being united to God she has stature and distance. A lofty eminence allows her a view which reaches out to more people. She benefits many, in imitation of her Spouse who has impressed on her heart the imprint of supernatural love.

Virgins are like flowers picked as soon as they bloom and placed on the altar. A virgin sings of the nobility of the human soul made for heaven, that heaven where we shall not be as much like man or woman as like angels.

To get an idea of how beautiful the state of virginity is, it suffices to ponder God's esteem for it.

In the course of centuries of Church history, when the Lord had a secret to reveal to humanity, very often he turned to virgins as the most trustworthy confidantes to transmit a message or make known his desire. They have been like antennas monitoring the divine. Sacrifice and love have made them particularly sensitive. Handmaids of the Lord, like a "new Mary," they have transmitted God's gift to others through the Church.

That Silence
of Yours

I Have Met You

I have met you in such different places,
Lord.
I've heard your heartbeat
in the deep stillness
of a mountain chapel,
in the dim light
of an empty cathedral's sanctuary lamp,
and in the unanimous aspiration
of a crowd that loves you,
and fills the arches of your church
with love and song.
I have met you in joy.
I have spoken with you
beyond the empyrean of the stars,
while I came home from work
in the evening, in silence.

I seek you, and find you often.
But where I always find you
is in pain.
Any pain whatsoever
is like the sound of a bell
summoning God's spouse to prayer.

When the shadow of the cross approaches,
the soul recollects herself
in her secret tabernacle,
oblivious of the ringing of the bell
she "sees" you and talks to you.
You have come to my door,
I have come to answer:
"I'm here, Lord, it's you who I want,
it's you I long for."
At this encounter
my soul,
all but inebriated with your love,
does not feel its pain,
I suffused with you, carrying you within me:
I in you, you in me,
that we may be one.
Then I reopen my eyes to life,
to the less true life,
using all you have taught me
for the battle to be waged in your name.

Thousands of Splendid Pearls

I am dreaming of a golden city.
There, what stands out is divine,
glistening with its own light,
and what is human forms a background,
it has retreated into the shadow,
so as the other's splendor
may shine the more.
Every church and tabernacle
outshines the sun,
for what reposes there
is the Love of all loves.
In the soul of those
who stand for the Church
(the hierarchy that structures the divine
    society planted on earth from heaven),
I see thousands of splendid pearls,

the graces deposited by God,
through the Virgin's hands,
into that channel whose only purpose is
to quench my thirst for light and nourish me
    with honey from heaven—
better than the most sublime earthly mother
    could nourish her child.
If I am recollected in God
and open the Book of Life
to read the eternal words,
then I sense in my soul
the shimmering harmony of song,
and the radiance of God's Spirit
    showering his gifts on me.
Whomever I meet,
noble-looking or disheveled,
I notice transfigured
by the beautiful face of the Incarnate Word,
Light from the Light.
On entering the home of persons
    who live in mutual love,
or of families united in Christ,
I glimpse the Trinity divinely reflected,
my ears catch the word "God,"
the word that is life,
manifested by that community.
God is my city's gold,

compared with him the sun is obscured,
the sky shrinks,
the beauty and majesty of nature retreats,
happy to re-form like a crown around him,
to serve him like a frame.
This city can be found in every city,
we could all see it,
provided our soul switches itself off in God,
forgetting everything else,
and switches on, inside,
the fire of God's love.

Inconceivable

It's inconceivable, extraordinary,
it's something which affects me
more and more deeply:
how you stay there silently in the tabernacle.
I come into church in the morning,
and there you are.
When I feel my love for you,
I run to the church,
and find you.
I stop in by chance or by habit
or out of respect,
and find you.
Each time you have something to tell me,
to correct some emotion;
what you are really doing is composing
in a variety of notes

a single song,
which my heart has memorized,
reiterating the one phrase:
eternal love.
O Lord,
you could not have invented anything better.
That silence of yours,
where the noise of our lives lowers its level;
that silent throb,
which wipes up all our tears;
that silence
resonating more powerfully than
    angelic choirs;
that silence
which utters the Word to our mind
and gives our heart a divine salve;
that silence
in which every voice finds acceptance
and every prayer feels transformed;
that inscrutable presence of yours—
that is where life is,
that is where you are waiting;
there our little heart finds rest,
then to resume, without delay, our journey.

My Time Is Fast Slipping Away

My time is fast slipping away,
accept my life, O Lord!
I keep you in my heart,
You are the treasure that must shape
    my every movement.
Be the one to look after me,
watch over me,
be my way to love:
both my enjoyment of life
and my suffering of pain.
Let nobody catch me heaving a sigh.
While hiding in your tabernacle
I live and work for everybody.
May the touch of my hand be yours,
and yours the tone of my voice.
May your love use me wretched as I am

to return into this parched world with the
    water that gushes copiously, Lord,
    from your wounded side.
O divine Wisdom, cheer up the gloom
    in so many sad people,
in all people.
Let Mary shine splendidly upon them.

A Divine Seed

The reason why Jesus did not stay on earth was so that he could live everywhere on earth in the eucharist. Being God, a divine seed as it were, he has borne fruit by multiplying his presence.

Like him, we too must die to multiply.

A Silent Song

When unity with others is complete, when difficulties have made it blossom with new flowers, as night fades into rising day and tears into light, it is then, O Lord, that I frequently find you.

Reentering the temple of my soul, I meet you there. Or, as soon as circumstances allow me to be alone, you invite me, you draw me, gently but firmly into your divine presence.

Then you alone reign, inside and outside of me, and this house that you have given me on the pilgrimage of life I feel to be, and call, the dwelling place of my God.

This presence of yours is love, but a love the world does not know.

My soul seems submerged in a delicious nectar, and my heart the cup that holds it. The whole soul is a silent song which no one hears but you: A melody that reaches your ears because it issues from you and is composed of you.

These are moments when peace can almost be touched, when I am certain of my salvation. Although still here on earth, I seem to be sailing in heaven. How strange to human intelligence, that although we have been busy with our neighbor all day long, in the evening we find the Lord. Every trace and memory of the created dissolves in him.

We don't seem to need faith at these moments, faith in God's existence. Gently penetrating our home, God becomes our portion and our inheritance, and he himself tells of his existence.

Christ Will Be My Cloister

I do not believe there is a man's heart, much less a woman's, which has never, not even once, felt the attraction of the cloister, especially in their youth.

The attraction is not to a cloistered form of life, but to something which seems to be concentrated there, between its four walls, beaming out a call heard even from afar.

Thanks to God, his light is present in communities scattered all over the world like constellations in the night sky. This presence strikes one as alive, because it has blossomed in the setting of real people who have wished to sacrifice their own poor image in the dark, for love of the Lord.

These homes of people united in God are plunged in silence. But through the mysterious power of the celestial they talk to human hearts in a voice with which the world is unacquainted, the beatitude of the union with God that human nature craves.

Yet, even my own home can have the aroma of the cloister; the walls of my abode can enclose a realm of peace, a divine fortress in the midst of the world.

It is not so much the external noise of the neighbors' radio turned on uninterruptedly that robs my home of its charm, or the noise of traffic outside, or the yelling of street vendors; rather, it is all the noise inside of me, turning my house into a public square, unprotected by walls because unprotected by love.

The Lord lives within me. He would like to be the one to inspire my every deed, the one to permeate my thought with his light, igniting my will: in other words, to guide me in my journey and my rest.

It is sometimes my ego that gets in the way. If that ceases to disturb me, the Lord himself will take possession of my whole existence and be able to give even these walls the air of an abbey and to this room the sacred feel of a church, to my sitting at table the gentleness of a ritual, to my clothing the perfume of a blessed habit, to the doorbell or the telephone the joyful note of a gathering with others which interrupts, yet continues, my conversation with God.

Then in the silence of self an Other will speak, and as I switch myself off a light will come on. It will shine far and wide, passing beyond these walls, almost consecrating them, while they protect a member of Christ, a temple of the Holy Spirit. Others will come to my house to join in seeking the Lord; in our joint loving search the flame will grow, the divine melody will raise its tone. My heart, though stuck in the midst of the world, will ask for nothing more. Christ will be my cloister, Christ in my heart, Christ in the midst of many hearts.

The Tiny Seed

Have you ever noticed a little blade of
grass, caressed by the winds of
spring, that has broken through
the surface of an abandoned road?
Life is reborn. It's insuppressible.
And it is the same in the humanity
surrounding you,
if you're careful not to look at it
through worldly eyes,
but restore it with charity's divine rays.
The supernatural love from your heart is
sunshine, which permits no
postponement to life's return.
It is a life that forms the cornerstone
for your own corner in life.
Nothing more is needed to pick the world

up and restore it to God.
Eloquence and polished manners,
the glitter of artistic talent,
heaps of education,
and years of experience,
are certainly not gifts to despise.
But, for the eternal kingdom,
what has more *life* in it has more value.
Take a tasty slice of a ripe apple,
it has lovely scent and color.
But bury it, and it will decay,
leaving no trace.
A tiny seed is not so pleasing to the palate,
it's nothing to look at, or to taste,
but bury it,
and it will grow fresh apples.
It is the same with life in God,
a Christian's life,
and the radiant journey of the Church.
Tall and majestic, she rests upon pillars
        that for ages have been called senseless,
        foolish, even insane . . . ;
the fury of the prince of this world
        was unleashed against them,
to destroy them down to the last trace.
They withstood.
The Father cleansed them

so that remaining attached to the vine
    they might bear abundant fruit.
He raised them to glory
in the kingdom of life.
You and I and the dairyman,
the migrant worker or the doorman,
the news vendor
or the fishermen and day laborers . . .
And all the others: disillusioned idealists,
overworked mothers,
lovers at the threshold of their wedding day,
exhausted old ladies waiting for death,
restless youth, all of them . . .
They are all prime material
for the city of God;
all they need is a heart,
aiming the flame of its love
tall and straight into God.

Perhaps More Beautiful Still

The Warhorse

Do you give the horse his strength,
and endow his neck with splendor?
Do you make the steed to quiver
while his thunderous snorting spreads terror?
He jubilantly paws the plain
and rushes in his might against the weapons.
He laughs at fear and cannot be deterred;
he turns not back from the sword.
Around him rattles the quiver,
flashes the spear and the javelin.
Frenzied and trembling he devours the ground;
he holds not back at the sound of the trumpet,
but at each blast cries, "Aha!"
Even from afar he scents the battle,
the roar of the chiefs and the shouting.
(Job 39:21-25)

If we read God's description of certain animals in the Old Testament scriptures, we realize that no poet or painter has sung of them or painted them so splendidly and vividly.

It took the vision of the Person who created them to inspire such majestic descriptions. Maybe our eye has not been schooled to recognize beauty or only sees the beauty of certain sectors of human and natural life, because we have not educated our souls.

Nature so rich in the traces of God surrounds the peasant girl. Yet she comes into town dressed in clothes so outlandish that their disharmony wounds the eye. To her, they are beautiful, but the greatest works of art mean little if anything to her, because she does not understand them.

From God's point of view, what is the most beautiful? A baby that stares at you with little innocent eyes, so similar to pure nature and so alive? Or the girl that glows with the freshness of a barely opened flower? Or the little old lady, white-haired and withered, bent over, incapable of doing almost anything, looking forward perhaps to nothing but death?

A grain of wheat, smaller than a blade of grass, clinging with its fellow grains to the ear they surround and compose, is so full of promise. It is just waiting for the moment when it will ripen. Then it will be released, independent and on its own, in the farmer's hand or deep in the ground, still beautiful and very hopeful.

It is beautiful yet, after ripening, if it is picked out as most suitable for being buried and giving life to new ears, life it already contains. How magnificent to be chosen for future generations of harvests!

But perhaps the grain is still more beautiful when, buried and shriveled underground, it is reduced to something so tiny and concentrated. It rots away in slow death, in order to give life to a tiny plant, other than itself, that carries the seed's life within it.

There are a variety of beauties.

Yet one is more beautiful than another.

And the last is the most beautiful of all.

Does God see things this way?

A beauty that we do not understand is in the wrinkles furrowing the forehead of a little old lady, and in her bent and trembling gait, her brief words charged with experience and wisdom, her gentle look as of both baby and woman combined, but with more goodness than only the one or the other.

This beauty of old age is a grain of wheat which, dying, is about to burst into new life, different from the former life, in new heavens.

I think this is the way God sees things. The final approach to heaven is far and away more attractive than any other step in life, whose lengthy path ultimately serves only for the opening of that final door.